MW00959067

THE
UNSTOPPABLE
ATHLETE

12 Keys to Unlock Your Full Potential
[The Only One Who Can Stop You, Is You]

Mindset, Confidence, & Peak Performance Habits
For Teen & College Athletes Who Play Sports

ANDREW J SIMPSON

Get 5 Big Bonuses, Become UNSTOPPABLE!

✓ The Unstoppable Athlete Downloadable
Action Guide
✓ The Unstoppable Athlete *Parent Edition*
✓ The 3 Keys to Mastering Your
Mindset Presentation
✓ Mental Reset Tool for In-Games
✓ The Advanced Goal Setting Workshop
for Serious Athletes

All FREE as a thank you for reading the book!
Scan the QR Code Below to get Access

Get The Entire Athlete Success Book Trilogy

PARENT EDITION of The Unstoppable Athlete: A Guide for Parents to Be Maximally Supportive In Helping Their Athletes Unlock for Potential http://parent.unstoppableathletebook.com

The Youth Truth: A Proven Playbook for Coaches and Parents to Develop Confident, Healthy, Wildly Successful Athletes without Adding Pressure or Pushing Them Away from Sports

ATHLETE! 7 Mindset Hacks to Dominate in Sports and Life: Proven Strategies for Teen and College Athletes to Stop Overthinking, Get Out of Their Head, and Finally Master Their Mindset

Dedication

This book is dedicated to Daniela, Jack, Giuliana, and Leo. The four of you are my inspiration each and every day to write and share encouragement, truth, and love with families and young athletes all over the world.

Table of Contents

Foreword
by Todd Durkin

I met Andrew Simpson in October of 2014 when he attended my 3.5 Day Mentorship program, and right away I knew he was special. At the time, he was a 24-year-old new business owner and had just opened up an athlete performance gym called Player's Fitness and Performance (PFP) in Frederick, MD. Although he was new to business, I could sense his energy and passion as he stood out as a leader in that group. He spoke well, asked insightful questions, and at one point, he came up and shared with me that he had an intention to join my "Power of 10" Mastermind group. My "Power of 10" was a group of high-level business owners that I personally coached and poured into as they created a massive impact in the fitness industry. Andrew's intention to step up into a group of much more experienced business owners was impressive, and it showed me the kind of person he was.

Through the years, I've gotten to know Andrew on a much deeper level, and the more I've worked with him, the more I've learned that he is a faith-centered, compassionate, lead-from-the-front kind of leader. When he knows what he wants, he has focus and dedication to getting it done like no one else I know. And I love the mission he and his team have to help student-athletes reach their full potential as athletes, and more importantly, as people.

In 2016, I visited his facility in Maryland to meet his team and see his mission in action. When I walked into his facility and met his staff, I felt the same passion and energy towards the cause they were fighting for that I did whenever I spoke with Andrew. This was not just a mission statement on a website–Andrew and his team were fully engaged as love-powered coaches and mentors to the young athletes who came in their doors.

On the surface, PFP helps athletes get bigger, faster, and stronger so that they can get to the next level. However, when you look beneath, you find there is something deeper. Much deeper. Everything that Andrew and his team does is intentional – they are committed to creating generational transformation and raising up leaders. PFP combines mindset with physical performance training. In addition, Andrew's books, his blog, and the online platform he and his team have built are all focused on holistic development of the student-athlete, and they all support his mission to help these young athletes stay on track and succeed...on the field and off.

In 2018, we had a special guest speaker at our mastermind retreat in California—Drew Brees, a former NFL legend and future Hall-of-Fame quarterback. I've been coaching and training Drew for almost 20 years, and I wanted to bring him in to share his insights and wisdom as an athlete, father, and friend. When I opened it up for Q&A at the end of the talk, Andrew immediately raised his hand.

"Drew, I know you are passionate about helping young athletes reach their full potential. We both know that young athletes need so much help and support right now, mentally and physically. The pressure to be great is more intense than ever before. I have this high school athlete who is incredibly talented but is struggling with anxiety and major self-doubt. Do you have any advice or encouragement for him that I could bring back to him and say it was from you?"

In the moment when he had an opportunity to ask any question at all, Andrew asked something to benefit one of his own athletes. That is the kind of man he is! He is committed to learning, creating, and doing whatever it takes to help athletes become *unstoppable!*

And that's what you're going to find out as you read this book. The 12 "keys" he shares—from creating a game plan to alleviate stress, anxiety and injury to tips on how to "get your mind right,"— are all massively important concepts and are guaranteed to help you play better in the game on the court or field... and also in the game of life! These 12 "keys" have been tried and tested and are guaranteed to help you reach your greatest potential!

So, without waiting any more, turn the page and start reading!

It's time to become UNSTOPPABLE!

Let's GO!

Todd Durkin, MA, CSCS
Author, Speaker, Life-Transformation Coach
Podcast, Todd Durkin IMPACT SHOW
Founder, Fitness Quest 10 & IMPACT-X Performance
2 Time Trainer of the Year (IDEA & ACE) &
Top 10 Gym in the U.S. (Men's Health; 2009 & 2010)
2018 Jack LaLanne Lifetime Legacy Award Winner

Introduction

un·stop·pa·ble
/ˌənˈstäpəb(ə)l/

adjective
    impossible to stop or prevent. unbeatable.

What does it truly mean to be unstoppable in sports? Picture yourself on the field, court, or track, hearing the resounding cheers of the crowd as they declare, "He just can't be stopped!" or "She is UNSTOPPABLE!"

Every athlete dreams of reaching this pinnacle of success, of being the force that cannot be contained or overcome.

But here's the harsh reality: very few athletes actually achieve this level of dominance. You want to be unstoppable in every play, every game, every tournament, and every race. And it's safe to assume that you don't want anything to stop your pursuit of your big dreams- you want to perform at a high level for long enough to break records.

Yet, despite these aspirations, many athletes find themselves stopped short of their goals. The problem? Most athletes are unaware of the mistakes, limiting mindsets, and bad habits that are holding them back from reaching their full potential.

Most athletes mistakenly think that if I "just work harder" I will become unstoppable. This is unfortunately not true. In order to be unstoppable, you'll need to do a lot more than just work harder. In fact, working harder may be the very thing that stops you!

To become unstoppable, you'll need to:

- Have an iron-clad game plan to beat competition anxiety, manage stress, and avoid major injuries.
- Unlearn the lies you've been fed about rest and achievement.
- Learn and develop habits of high performing, healthy, happy, mentally tough athletes.
- Learn how to master your mindset in games and competitions.
- Think long-term about your career and success.
- Sharpen your axe, be consistent, and raise your intensity.
- Balance patience and persistence.
- Keep your passion high for long enough to become the best you can be.
- Maximize your ultradian rhythms to stay fresh and at the top of your game.

By picking up this book, you're gaining an invaluable advantage. You're about to uncover the secrets to becoming unstoppable.

Imagine if I told you that the greatest athletes on the planet approach their craft in a completely different manner than 99.9% of athletes your age. It's true! This book serves as your playbook to becoming an athlete who cannot and will not be stopped. It's your guide to achieving peak performance while maintaining your happiness, health, and drive.

There are numerous factors that can impede your progress: mental blocks, fear-driven motivation, pressure handling, loss of passion, laziness, overuse injuries, and more. Many of these are within your control, yet most athletes either ignore them or fail to take action to address them. Are you ready to build the right mindset and habits to overcome these obstacles?

It's time to confront your challenges head-on, just like a champion. You must discipline yourself to balance patience and persistence consistently over time. This is the key to gradually ascending to the peak of your game.

Too often, athletes reach the next level only to find themselves questioning their own mindset and ability to handle pressure. You don't want to be that athlete. You don't want to feel like your efforts are never enough, constantly working harder to meet ever-increasing expectations.

This book is for the athlete who gives their all to their sport but still feels like they're falling short. It contains the essential message you need to hear on your journey to long-term success: you can achieve greatness, break records, and reach your full potential with less stress, less fear, and fewer injuries. Sounds enticing, doesn't it?

However, if you read this book and then choose to follow the crowd, you'll inevitably get lost in it. You won't stand out, and you won't achieve the level of success you know you're capable of. Throughout these pages, we'll debunk the lies and myths that hold young athletes back from success. We'll identify common rookie mistakes and provide strategies to overcome them.

But most importantly, we'll study the habits and secrets of Olympic and professional athletes who have reached the top of their game while maintaining their passion, a life outside of sports, and their physical and mental well-being.

Have you ever wondered how athletes like Tom Brady or LeBron James have sustained their success over decades? In this book, you'll learn the elite athlete secrets that set them apart from the rest. Warning: as you read on, you'll be challenged to think differently. You may find yourself questioning how others will view you if you dare to break from the norm. Don't let those doubts hold you back. To become an unstoppable athlete, you must embrace the path less traveled.

This is your moment – your moment to be courageous. The path to becoming an elite athlete is narrow, and even narrower is the path to achieving greatness while maintaining your health and happiness. Don't dwell on the past or worry about the future. Focus on controlling today's controllables and forging your own path forward.

In the upcoming chapters, you'll learn from the experiences of athletes like Sonya, who struggled with time and energy management but ultimately thrived. Our daily habits shape our results in life, and Sonya's journey serves as a reminder of the transformative power of effective scheduling and prioritization.

Get ready to embark on your journey to becoming unstoppable. It won't be easy, but it will be worth it. Let's learn from the past, seize the present, and shape the future of our athletic careers together.

KEY #1

Do NOT Be Stopped: Your Game Plan Against Stress, Anxiety, and Injury

Sonya is a high-level high school swimmer. You may relate to her story.

She looked miserable as she walked into my office for a Mindset Session. Just so you understand what I am talking about, I am the founder of an athlete training gym called Player's Fitness and Performance as well as the creator of a mental performance program called the Mindset Performance Academy.

Usually, we start the session with a great exercise for any athlete. We reflect on the question, "What's been GREAT this past month? What are some wins, some highlights, some areas of progress?" But on this day, I didn't see a need. Sonya was exhausted and looking distraught.

"You look tired," I said to her.

"Yeahhh. You could say that. But I placed top 5 in my swim meet!" she said to me with fake enthusiasm.

The dopamine hit of placing top 5 had already worn off, as it so often does after an *achievement*.

All that was left was reality.

Sonya's Schedule

Monday-Thursday

-   Wake up at 5 am to drive 45 minutes to her new school that she was attending that would give her a better chance at a D1 soccer scholarship.
-   Practice with the team (offseason "optional" training) from 6-7 am
-   Shower at school, eat a muffin and banana.
-   Classes from 8 am- 3 pm
-   Swim practice from 3:30 pm - 5:30 pm
-   Mom picks her up and they drive home in traffic from 5:45 pm- 7 pm
-   Dinner from 7:15-7:45 pm
-   Shower around 8 pm
-   Homework from 8:30-10:30 pm
-   And of course, she's human, she gets distracted multiple times. Her brain is fried from a full day, so it naturally wants to do the easiest, less stressful thing– scroll social media.

Wednesdays specifically

-   Same as above except swim ends at 5 pm, so that opens the door for soccer skill practice from 7 pm-8 pm (they drive straight from school to soccer skills).
-   This bumps everything back 1 hour and Sonya gets to sleep by 11:30 pm on Wednesdays.

Fridays

- No morning practice with the soccer team, hooray! Sleep in till 6 am (which gives her ~7 hours of sleep)
- School from 8 am - 3 pm
- Lifting from 3:30 pm - 5 pm
- Stay at school at watch a varsity sports game with her friends.
- Get home around 8 pm and receive pressure from dad to do a little juggling in the basement ("Sonya, while your competition is resting you could be getting better," he nudges her with a soft pressure that causes Sonya to fear falling behind *and* letting her dad down).

Saturdays

- Club soccer tournaments or showcases almost every weekend.
- On off-weekends, her schedule is always loaded up with something soccer or training related.

Sundays

- Same as Saturday, tournaments and/or skill work

I am sure you can feel Sonya's pain when you look at her schedule! Sonya was stressed, anxious, and deteriorating.

Stressed.

Her grades were suffering. *"I'll never get a scholarship with grades like this. Mom and dad always tell me that college coaches care MOST about my grades. This is confusing, though. Why do they say that but then push me to do more with my sport?"*

Her assignments were piling up. *"This is getting heavy. I feel like the weight of the world is pushing down on me."*

The words she used, "heavy, pushing down on me" created even more stress for Sonya. Did you know that your words can actually intensify your emotions?

Her friends never saw her. *Social stress.* *"What if I end up with no real friends and no one liking me?"*

Not all stress is bad stress. As an athlete who wants to achieve big dreams, you need to put your body through stressful situations and push past discomfort.

The "bad stress" is the kind that results when you have an overfull plate and are spreading yourself too thin. Bad stress happens when we start giving up what we want *most* for what we want *now.*

Throughout this book I will help you figure out your priorities *so that* you can make sure you are not sacrificing the most important things for short-term wins. Because, if you do that long enough, you will be stopped and you will never reach your full potential.

Bad stress is the result of you operating out of fear rather than faith. That is what Sonya was doing.

Anxious.

"Am I enough? Am I doing enough? Am I missing out? Will I have regrets?"

Sonya was in a chronic state of *anxiety and worry.*

Oftentimes, parents will add to this anxiety inadvertently by sharing stories about *themselves* as athletes and how they "could've, should've, and would've" if only they had worked harder, been more disciplined, sacrificed more, etc.

This encouragement has its time, place, and benefits, but for most athletes, this just adds to the stress, doesn't it?

Being anxious is usually the result of one of two things:

A) You choose to go against your values (things that matter most) even though you know better.
You overload your plate and try to be superman or supergirl, even though you know you've reached your limit. Sonya had reached her limit but ignored those feelings of burnout, even though she knew something needed to change.

B) Your focus.
Control your focus, control your emotions.
When I focus on the negative outcome that *might* happen in the future, I become anxious. I

can take deep breaths and that may help, but the moment I re-focus on something that could go wrong or has gone wrong, the anxious thoughts will come back.

But what happens when you choose to focus on the times in your past where you succeeded?

What do you feel when you reflect on your victories?

If you want to become unstoppable, you must beat your worries and anxieties by choosing to focus on the good rather than the bad.

Deteriorating.

"She's been swimming so well, Andrew," her mom said to me. She has PR'd in almost every single race!

"How's she holding up physically?" I asked.

"Well, her shoulders are bothering her a good bit, but we haven't had time to see a PT (shocker) and it shouldn't really affect her in soccer since she's a striker."

Did she just say that?!?

Sonya was deteriorating. The definition of deteriorating is *becoming progressively worse.*

The problem with deterioration is that *it happens without you even noticing it.*

One moment, one practice, one session, one day at a time. It almost isn't noticeable, especially for you and for the people who see you every day. It's why *I* was able to see it clearly, but mom, dad, and Sonya could not.

In my book *The Youth Truth: Coaching and Parenting in Today's CRAZY Youth Sports World*, I shared the ugly truth that injuries are at an all-time high and climbing among youth athletes. The number one cause is *overuse*, which we will discuss later on.

Sonya was stressed, anxious, and deteriorating physically. Have you ever felt like Sonya? Are you on the same path that Sonya was on? And if you don't decide to get onto a new path, are you going to end up where she did?

Most athletes think that excessive stress, anxiety, and injuries are just part of the game. "Pain is gain."

But that is not the way that elite, Hall of Fame athletes think about sports. In Chapter 3 we will look into one of the greatest athletes of all time to see how he keeps himself physically, mentally, and emotionally healthy while breaking records and being the best.

There is a better way, and that is what this book is all about.

A Secret to Unstoppable, Long-Term Success

Athlete, a "S.A.D." sports career will stop you from reaching the top of your game.

"You can't just hope for things to get better. You must change for things to get better."

Certain things don't just get better. We either decide to stop doing the things that are holding us back or we start doing the things that will propel us forward. We either model others who have gone before us and achieved what we want to achieve, or we choose to keep going our own way.

Here is a secret to LONG-TERM success: *Your desire to impress others, please them, and be significant will drive you to be successful in the long term, but that same thing will be what stops you from achieving peak potential long-term. You must choose to be a leader. You must decide today that you will lead yourself well, and you will not just do what everyone else is doing. You will make tough choices, do the hard things even when you don't feel like doing them, and you will think long-term.*

This is what leads to a S.A.D. sports career.

Athlete, you do not need to settle for a S.A.D. life. Stressed, anxious, and deteriorating athletes are everywhere. We don't need more of them. They may be the norm, but they don't need to be *your norm*.

You can achieve great things *and* have a balanced life. Do not settle for anything less.

An athlete that we have already mentioned and will talk about later on is LeBron James. At the time of this writing, LeBron is still going strong and showing absolutely no signs of slowing down in his 21st year in the league. Whether you like him or not is irrelevant. The guy is basically the definition of Unstoppable. From what we can tell, he has a healthy mindset and a great life. He rarely gets injured, he's broken the all-time scoring record, won 4 championships, and all because he has lasted long enough and kept his passion high enough to become the best version of himself.

If that is what you want, too, keep reading.

PAUSE AND REFLECT:

List out your current weekly schedule in the space below. Include school, practice, games, and other consistent events that are a part of your weekly routine.

Be specific with the times that these things typically start and end.

Example

Sunday	Monday	Tuesday	Wednesday	Thursday	Friday	Saturday
Club practice from 10 am-1 pm OR Tournaments all day	6 am wake up 7 am- 3 pm school 3:30 pm-5:30 pm practice 6 pm get home, shower, eat dinner 7:30 pm start homework 9 pm get on social media 11 pm go to bed	6 am wake up 7 am- 3 pm school 3:30 pm-5:30 pm practice 6 pm-7 pm workout 7:30 pm get home, shower, eat dinner 9 pm start homework 11 pm go to bed	6 am wake up 7 am- 3 pm school 3:30 pm-5:30 pm practice 6-7 pm hitting with private coach 7:30 pm get home, shower, eat dinner 9 pm start homework 11 pm go to bed	6 am wake up 7 am- 3 pm school 3:30 pm-5:30 pm practice 6 pm-7 pm workout 7:30 pm get home, shower, eat dinner 9 pm start homework 11 pm go to bed	6 am wake up 7 am- 3 pm school 3:30 pm-5:30 pm practice 6:30 pm go watch the football/basketball game with friends 8 pm go to the movies/hangout 1 am bed	8 am wake up 8-9 am Workout at the gym Practice from 11-1 pm OR Tournaments all day
Total Sleep	7 hours	7 hours	7 hours	7 hours	7 hours	

1. How many days throughout the week do I truly have OFF from my sport? _____

2. How many days through the week do I get LESS than 8 hours of sleep? _____ *(8 hours is the number of hours that researchers have confirmed through DNA testing that 90% of the population absolutely needs for peak mental and physical performance, and to have a better chance at avoiding certain health issues.)*

3. Which day of the week COULD I truly have off from all things sports related? _____

4. How many hours through the week do I have for true family time? _____

5. What activities/hobbies/important things am I NOT able to do right now because of the way my schedule is?

   Examples: *Recovery, Family, Hobbies, Relationships, Church, Studying, etc.*

6. Do I take pride in my busy schedule? Is it a "badge of honor" for me? If so, why do I do that?

7. What are the biggest opportunities in my schedule? What can I change TODAY to make my schedule better reflect my values and give me more time to rest and recover?

Sunday	Monday	Tuesday	Wednesday	Thursday	Friday	Saturday
Total Sleep						

Now, before we get into the habits of the best athletes in the world, we need to address the most common lies that are holding you back from being unstoppable.

KEY #2

Run Your Own Race: Ignore the 3 Lies That Increase Pressure and Fear

There is a very clear line between being lazy, and overworking/stressing yourself out because of the fear of falling behind, not measuring up, and not living up to expectations.

In this chapter we are going to call out the three big lies that are causing you to underperform in the short term while also crushing your joy and passion on your journey to reaching your full potential. These three lies sound good, but make no mistake, they are inhibiting your success.

Again, this chapter is *not* about being lazy. Laziness will not get you to the top of your game. It may get you to the top of the leaderboard in Minecraft, but it won't help you reach your athletic dreams. This chapter is about knowing when to pull back and when to push forward.

The Lies Unsuccessful Athletes Believe

1. *"More is better. Want to get the edge on competition? Train more. Train harder. Rest when you are dead."*

Now, I am not saying don't work hard. This is an absolute must. However, *more* is NOT always better.

Do you ever assess the effectiveness of your gym workout on whether or not you got absolutely crushed during the session?

I understand the temptation and attractiveness of gauging your progress on how awful you feel after a workout or practice. Many coaches have reduced mental toughness down to *"Did you push yourself hard enough that you threw up? If not, it wasn't good enough."*

But have you ever stopped and asked if this actually makes sense or not? Are there *other* markers of effectiveness during training that are equally important?

Have you ever stopped to ask yourself, "What is winning to me? What IS success for me?"

If you want to be unstoppable and soar to the top of your game, you'll need to remain healthy, happy, and passionate. If this is how you become unstoppable, then the "more is better" mindset is definitely the wrong path to get there.

Elite athletes like Roger Federer (Tennis), Usain Bolt (Track and Field- Fastest Man in History), and Michael Phelps (Swimmer- Most Decorated Olympian in History) all understood this. They trained hard but kept balance in their lives and made sure that rest, renewal (mentally and physically), and recovery were always a big part of their journey. They were different.

But that makes sense, right?

You wouldn't expect the best athletes in the universe to *do what everyone else does.*

It wouldn't make sense that the top 1% would have the same routines as the bottom 99%.

2. *"Never be satisfied."*

This one sounds good on the surface as well, and we can see the motivational value.

But the problem with this one is that it's incomplete. It is *close* to being helpful, but because it's missing the full story, and therefore it's unhelpful.

You see, the "author" of this idea was trying to communicate that you should never allow yourself to be *complacent*. You should always keep growing, improving, evolving.

YES! Amen! I am with you on that!

But that's not the way our sports society has taken this message. At all.

Here is a better approach:

"Do NOT allow yourself to become complacent, but DO give yourself the gift of satisfaction."

Athlete, how does a sports career where you were never satisfied sound?

Miserable. A lack of satisfaction consistently stops athletes from being the best they can be.

How does it feel to get a "Great job, you are really making progress. I am proud of you" from a coach?

Pretty good, right? Almost like you feel *unstoppable?*

I bet it even motivates you to work harder.

The myth that tells us to "never be satisfied" has zero benefit in the *long-term.*

Be satisfied when you know you have worked hard and are making progress. Give yourself that gift.

3. If I rest, then "they" will leapfrog me.

Anytime you have a thought or statement that includes, "If/then", your internal warning alarm should sound!

Motivation that comes from fear doesn't last, it doesn't produce peak performance, and it will not result in feeling joy or peace in the process.

Think about a boss who tells an adult, "if you don't hit your numbers, you will get demoted". If you don't do _____, then _____ will happen.

It is a motivational technique that works in the short-term, but it fails the test of integrity in the long-term.

A wise person once said, "There is no love in fear."

The moment you let fear become your driving motivation is the moment that you begin losing your love for the game.

We make silly choices when we are motivated by fear.

- We play on a broken ankle (which is very different from playing through a cold or low grade fever).
- We train for 3 hours even though our ultradian rhythms (I will explain this concept later on) and our body clearly told us after 90 minutes that our returns were being diminished exponentially and we were beginning to metabolize our own muscle to fuel our workouts.
- We cheat, we lie, we hurt ourselves, and we hurt others like our teammates when we are motivated by fear.

The truth is that "they," whoever "they" are, might leapfrog you anyway. You might as well keep yourself healthy, passionate, and energized so that you can sustain your drive long enough to become the best you can be.

There were *moments* that Tom Brady got beat by other quarterbacks. What did he do?

He stayed focused on his long-term goals and his gameplan. He trained, he recovered, he ate healthy, he studied, and he became the greatest quarterback in history. No one remembers the moments where the other QB won. They remember his legacy. They remember the majority. They remember that Tom was the last man standing.

Stay in Your Lane

In the 2012 Olympics, Chad Le Clos beat Michael Phelps by .05 seconds to win the gold medal in the 200 meter butterfly.

Four years later in their much anticipated rematch at the 2016 Rio Olympics, Michael Phelps regained the gold beating out Le Clos by .7 seconds.

In the final 50 meters of the close race, a photographer snapped an iconic photo that every single athlete on the planet needs to see and learn from.

Le Clos was caught looking over at Phelps, while Phelps had his eyes on the prize. Google this, it is fascinating.

If you focus on another athlete leapfrogging you, you will get leapfrogged.

If you focus on what you can control, you will be successful.

Success: *having peace of mind and self-satisfaction knowing that I did all I could do to be the best I could be.*

"More is better."

"Never be satisfied."

"If I rest, then I will be leapfrogged."

These are three of the biggest, most common lies that our achievement addicted society shouts to us and our athletes.

By now, you can see these lies for what they are, but you can also see that these lies have shaped the way you view and do sports. At least to some degree.

And it is going to take some serious diligence, intentionality, and effort on your part to shift your beliefs about achievement and rest. The pressures from society are huge and they are slowly, silently, subtly stopping you. They will crush your passion, joy, and confidence overtime.

Congratulations. You are in the early stages of creating a new mindset and a foundation to build on. You are ready to learn what it takes to be an uncommon, unstoppable athlete who thrives during your athletic journey.

PAUSE AND REFLECT

1. Which of the 3 lies have I believed?

2. What have been the negative consequences that those beliefs have resulted in?

3. What would it look like for me to be better at "staying in my lane?"

KEY #3

Implement the Habits of Mentally Tough, Healthy, Happy, High-Performing Athletes

Have you ever found yourself super focused on the problems you are facing, but not enough on the solutions to the problems?

"Why am I not getting as much playing time as I want!?"

"Why can't I hit the ball!"

"I keep messing up! I'm never going to make it!"

It could be that you are too focused on the results you *don't want*, and you are not focused enough on what you *do want*.

In the first chapter, we lasered in on what we want to *avoid*- we do not want to become a stressed, anxious, deteriorating athlete who became that way because of an unhealthy obsession with achievement, that was driven by the fear of not being enough, falling behind, and not living up to expectations.

But you can't just stop with a clear picture of what you *don't* want. Our brains are not good at filtering out the word "don't" when it exists by itself. This is a great thing to know as a parent or coach. Don't stop at "don't do _____".

Spend time thinking about the GOAL The TARGET. Think about what it *should* look like and talk about this 5x as often as you talk about the problem. This is a major key to you becoming unstoppable.

"Don't be stressed. Don't be anxious. Don't get injured. Don't mess up. Don't get distracted."

If those things are the *wrong* targets, then what is the *ideal* target we are after?

Mental toughness. Health (mental and physical). Happiness. High Performance.

What's wrong is always available. But so is what's right! We get what we focus on, so focus on the targets you want to HIT!

THE TARGETS:

1. Mentally tough

Every athlete wants to be mentally tough. Your coaches and parents have been encouraging you to be mentally tough for years.

But how do the best athletes in the world become mentally tough? Have you ever thought about that?

What are you currently doing to improve your mental toughness?

First, let's define mental toughness:

Mental toughness is your ability to handle setbacks, mistakes, challenges, and other types of adversity. The better you are able to deal with these types of challenges, the more mentally tough you are. Mentally tough people are able to see the good through any difficult situation.

By playing on more club teams, going to more showcases, and training harder, you are not necessarily improving your mental toughness. *Those things actually just REVEAL your current level of mental toughness.*

To become mentally tough, you need to:

1. Understand the way your brain actually works
2. Know why you do what you do and why you respond the way you respond
3. Learn how to shift your focus from negative to positive, from what you can't control to what you can
4. Be able to change your perspective in the moment by changing what you N.A.B. - what you notice, appreciate, and believe about the challenge in front of you
5. Create new definitions of success and failure, and what they each mean to you
6. Create new patterns of language and self-talk
7. Learn to visualize success in action, whatever that looks like for you

8. Practice being courageous and facing things that scare you
9. Be challenged on the way you currently think and act
10. Stand for what you believe is right, resist the urge to take the easy path, and choose to be uncommon.

You see, mental toughness is far more than running until you vomit or pushing yourself to play in a game with a 103 degree fever. Those may be *actions* that mentally tough people decide to do at times, but they are not what makes you a mentally tough individual.

What to become mentally tough? Study people who have walked through adversity and have become better because of it. Model athletes who lean into their challenges.

And if you are ready to take action and learn the 7 mindset hacks to become a more mentally tough athlete, grab my book *ATHLETE! I'm Talking To You.*

2. Healthy

LeBron James has played in 94% of possible games in his career, and he has never missed a playoff game. He has never played in fewer than 84% of one season's games.

Not to mention, you can count on him for a consistent 27 points, 7 rebounds, and 7 assists in 38 minutes per game.

We can learn a lot from the way he has applied his values to his priorities.

Here are LeBron's 7 priorities that help him stay healthy, physically and mentally:

1. **Rest and Recovery:** Sleep is a top priority for LeBron, and the research on sleep supports this. Athlete, are you getting 8+ hours of solid sleep each night?

In a 2018 interview, Lebron's former teammate Ivan Shumpert shared with Business Insider Magazine that "James prioritizes rest, recovery, and health over everything else."

In the same interview, Kevin Durant, an NBA Champion, MVP, and future hall of famer had this to say about LeBron's approach to rest and recovery: *"One thing I learned about LeBron is that he takes care of his body. He knows that in order for him to play that long, his body has to be up. He has to keep that in shape. Like, he works on his body, like, religiously."*

Still wondering how LeBron has performed at an insanely high level for more than two decades?

He does the slow, boring, easy to skip things, like icing *after* a game. That was the final thing that Shumpert was impressed by. "He puts that ice on right after the game — he gonna sit there."

Athlete, if you want to be great, you have to play long enough to become great. And if you want to play long enough to be great, you need to rest and recover more.

2. **Family Time**: Spending quality time with his wife and children is an essential aspect of his life outside of basketball.

How present are you with your family? Do you feel like you get enough quality time with each of your family members?

Perhaps taking 1 day off per week, or playing on just 1 team instead of 2, could free up more time for you to spend with the people you love. These are hard choices, but I believe in you, and I know you can do hard things. Sometimes you need to be brave enough to stop doing something that is *good*, so that you can get something back that is *great*.

3. **Business Ventures**: LeBron is actively involved in various business ventures off the basketball court. This includes his involvement in entertainment, production, and philanthropy.

His example shows us that having hobbies and interests outside of our sports will last longer and play with more passion than other athletes whose only focus is their sport.

"Ball is life" looks great on a t-shirt, but it's a recipe for a short, less than stellar career.

We will have fun discussing whether it is better to play one sport or multiple sports later on.

4. **Training and Fitness**: While LeBron values rest, he also maintains a commitment to his fitness. It's not always high-intensity workouts, although those do show up in his routine.

If his body needs low-intensity workouts, conditioning sessions, or other movement based exercises, he does them.

Do you prioritize strength and performance training throughout the entire year? Or are you barely squeezing in a few weeks of training during a short off season? Make small changes, don't beat yourself up.

5. **Giving Back, Making an Impact:** LeBron is known for his engagement in social activism and giving back. He uses his platform to advocate for social justice issues and contribute to various charitable causes.

We all know that the secret to living is giving. Are you experiencing the joy of giving back, athlete?

How can you start contributing to your community? How can you help younger athletes, or other players on your team, improve? Maybe, it starts with helping your siblings. What can you do to make a positive impact in their lives?

6. **Mental Preparation:** LeBron often speaks about the mental aspect of his game. His downtime may involve mental preparation, including visualization, mindfulness, and other techniques to stay mentally sharp.

Do you ever struggle with:

- Being in your head
- Not being present in games
- Perfectionism
- Sports anxiety
- Performing worse in games than you do in practice
- Obsessing over playing time and focusing on things you can't control
- Letting your emotions and frustrations get the best of you
- Holding back and playing passively because you are scared of failing.

If any of those are true for you, you are not alone. Most athletes struggle with these things.

But you don't have to struggle forever. You can decide today that you will create a mental preparation plan for sports. Like LeBron, you could start learning about mindset by reading books like this or watching videos. Or, you could even get your own Mindset Coach like the pros have.

7. **Hobbies:** LeBron likely engages in hobbies and activities that bring him joy and relaxation.

Do you have hobbies? Do you do things for fun that restores your passion and energy?

By now you should be encouraged. There are likely many things you can stop doing and start doing in order to become healthier! And once you have your health, you can finally be *happy*.

3. Happy

I define happiness as a deep and lasting sense of positivity and contentment that comes from knowing who you are, why you matter, and that you are *way more* than your grades and accolades.

Happiness comes when our inner life in consistent with your outer life. Have you ever found yourself faking your happiness in front of your friends, teammates, and coaches, but then when you are all alone and your head hits the pillow at night, you feel the reality of your unhappiness?

Too many athletes are managing their image rather than managing their energy and emotions. They are doing *all the things* to impress others and make others happy, but they themselves are not happy.

Impress → Improve

Happiness is about shifting from Impress to Improve. Im-press sounds a lot like "I'm Pressing" doesn't it? Pressing too hard leads to unhappiness.

Athlete, are you really happy?

Many people aren't. Many athletes are pursuing the scholarship or getting drafted, even though that alone will never bring them the satisfaction that they are hoping for.

Happiness comes from giving more than you get, knowing who you are, being content with what you have, and the confidence that comes from knowing that you are putting in your best effort.

Do you want to be happy?

Research shows that you do *not* have to arrive at the destination of "happiness" in order to experience the positive effects.

You just have to feel confident that you are actually *on the right path*. Progress is what you are after. You thrive on growth and progress.

If what you have been doing up to this point has led to more unhappiness than happiness, or roller-coaster happiness, don't you think it is time to do things differently?

That is what this book is about – doing things differently and getting different results.

4. High-Performing

I define high-performance as being able to set and reach your goals consistently while maintaining positive mental-well-being, high levels of energy, physical health, and relationships along the way. Anything short of this and you will likely be stopped.

If your definition of high-performance leaves any one of those things out of it, you'll eventually wish you didn't.

According to Brendon Burchard, the World's #1 Coach and Author on High-Performance, high performers have 5 things in common. He explains them in further detail in his book, *High Performance Habits.*

1. **Clarity**: High performers have a clear sense of who they are, what their goals are, and how they want to interact with others, such as their teammates and coaches. They are intentional about their goals and priorities, and they regularly review, reflect on, and refine their vision for the future.

After you assess yourself on a scale of 1-5 in the area of clarity, ask *"why"*? Why did I score what I scored?

2. **Energy**: High performers actively manage and optimize their energy levels. This includes physical energy through proper nutrition, exercise, and sleep, as well as emotional and mental energy through practices like mindfulness and stress management.

Remember Sonya? She achieved short-term success in swimming, but she was exhausted every day and never had energy for friends, homework, or other things that were important to her.

In his book, *The Power of Full Engagement*, authors Jim Loehr and Tony Schwartz shared scientific and anecdotal evidence that it is actually *not* time management, but rather *energy management*, that is the key to high performance and personal renewal.

We aren't much good to ourselves or our team if our energy stinks.

3. **Necessity**: Brendon Burchard says that high performers connect their daily activities to a sense of purpose and necessity. They approach tasks with a mindset that what they are doing is meaningful and important, aligning their actions with their values and long-term goals.

In order to reach your highest level of performance in anything (school, athletics, career, etc.) you are going to have to move beyond "it would be nice to", "I should", and "I could", to "*I MUST*".

Necessity is when you turn your *optionals* into *requirements*. The key is to avoid forcing the issue and becoming overly obsessed.

How do we raise our level of necessity but at the same time, not become addicted to the very thing we are trying to reach our highest level of performance in?

Best Practice: Get feedback from people who love you and want the best for you. When was the last time you asked someone who knows you and your goals the question, "What do you think I need to stop doing or start doing? Do I need to prioritize more recovery, better nutrition, more running? Do you think I need to give up this extra club team because it's forcing me to play 7 days a week?"

Who can you ask for feedback from today?

Higher levels of performance will require you to raise your level of necessity for BOTH success in your sports *as well as* success in the most important areas of your life. Remember, high-performance is about having both. And both will make you UNSTOPPABLE.

4. **Productivity**: High performers prioritize effectively, they set clear goals, and implement strategies to increase their efficiency and effectiveness in their efforts to achieve those goals.

High performing athletes say the word "no" more often than those who never quite perform at their full potential. This keeps them from burning out.

Many athletes today say "yes" to everything. They say yes to playing on the new team, getting another private instructor, and anything else that they see their teammates doing or that their coaches tell them to do. This is *not* what the best of the best do.

If you want to achieve your highest level of performance, before saying "yes" you must start asking the question, "When I think about my goals and what really is most important, are there other things I should prioritize that would help me? Or is this really the best thing I should spend my time on and say yes to right now?"

When you know the 20% of activities that lead to 80% of your results, you can actually do better at maintaining balance in your life! You can recover and rest more, have more time for hobbies, have more time for family, and you can have a life outside of sports. All without the fear of falling behind!

It's almost hard to believe, but the highest performing athletes in the world actually have the best balance in their lives because they aren't just busy being busy. They get really good at spending their best time on the things that matter most!

As an athlete, this means taking your strengths to the moon while you simultaneously get your weaknesses up to an acceptable baseline.

What do you do best in your sport? What is your best skill or ability?

What are your big goals? What do you need to prioritize more of in order to achieve those goals?

We have an entire Advanced Goal Setting Workshop that we take athletes through to help them clarify their most important goals and build a solid plan to achieve them. You can access that goal setting workshop for free along with your other bonuses.

5. **Influence**: Finally, high performers understand the importance of positively influencing others. They prioritize relationships, they seek to make a difference, and they demonstrate leadership qualities that inspire and motivate those around them.

When you decide that you want to be a person of influence, everything changes.

Once you get out of your head and past your stinkin' thinkin' that says, "I'm not loud enough to be a leader, that's not really me", you are then finally free to become the leader that you were created to be.

You can only sustain high-performance long-term if you embrace the role of being a leader.

The highest performing athletes are always learning, growing, and sharing what they know with others. It keeps them on their toes and is a key part of their ongoing motivation.

So, there you have it – mental toughness, health, happiness, *and* high-performance.

This entire book has been created to help you become that kind of athlete. When you know where and what the bullseye is, you can aim your dart at it. Focus on it long enough, and you WILL hit it.

PAUSE TO REFLECT

1. How healthy do I feel? Mentally, emotionally, spiritually, physically?
2. Why or why not?
3. How happy am I? Do I have joy inside of me that doesn't constantly go away when times get tough? Am I really enjoying life and sports to the fullest?
4. Why or why not?
5. How do I rate myself in each of the 5 areas of being a high performer?
   a. Clarity: /5
   b. Energy: /5
   c. Necessity: /5
   d. Productivity: /5
   e. Influence: /5
6. Which 2 from above do I want to be my biggest focus right now and why?

KEY #4

Play Multiple Sports, Develop More Skills

The majority of elite athletes who dominated in their sport over long, long periods of time and stayed healthy along the way, played multiple sports when they were growing up.

If you only play one sport, it *is* possible to sustain success long-term. However, if you are going to choose to specialize in one sport, it is going to take an insane amount of intentionality to avoid injury, burnout, and other challenges.

The reason you must be more intentional about these things is because there has been a bunch of research that shows athletes who specialize in one sport at a young age are far more likely to end up with injuries and mental health challenges.

Again, it's not impossible. There *have* been athletes who specialized early on, achieved greatness over a long period of time, and stayed healthy mentally and physically. But the number of athletes who fit into this category is very small. We will talk about that shortly.

For now, let's look into the facts:

The Link Between Injuries and Early Sport Specialization

American Journal of Sports Medicine (2015): A study found that young athletes who specialized in one sport were **1.5 times more likely to sustain an overuse injury than those who participated in multiple sports.**

International Journal of Sports Physical Therapy (2016): Research showed that **early sports specialization was a significant risk factor for overuse injuries** in young athletes, emphasizing the importance of diversified athletic experiences.

National Athletic Trainers' Association (NATA) (2017): NATA published a consensus statement highlighting the risks of **early sports specialization, noting that it contributes to a higher likelihood of overuse injuries, burnout, and emotional stress.**

Journal of Athletic Training (2018): A study found that athletes specializing in one sport **before the age of 12** had a higher risk of overuse injuries compared to those who engaged in multiple sports.

American Academy of Pediatrics (AAP) (2016): The AAP released a policy statement discouraging sports specialization before puberty, emphasizing the **increased risk of overuse injuries associated with early specialization.**

The Orthopaedic Journal of Sports Medicine (2019): A systematic review concluded that **early sports specialization was linked to a higher risk of overuse injuries in youth athletes**.

American Medical Society for Sports Medicine (AMSSM): Experts from AMSSM have emphasized that **early specialization is a key factor contributing to the rising rates of overuse injuries in youth sports**.

Journal of Science and Medicine in Sport (2019): Research indicated that athletes specializing in one sport were more likely to experience overuse injuries, **and these injuries were often more severe compared to those participating in multiple sports**.

British Journal of Sports Medicine (2018): A review article highlighted that early sports specialization was associated with an increased risk of overuse injuries, **particularly in the context of year-round training**.

American Journal of Sports Medicine (2021): A recent study found that young athletes specializing in one sport had a higher risk of overuse injuries, **with the intensity and duration of sports participation playing significant roles**.

*It appears that specializing in one sport early on leads to more injuries, and more injuries is one of the biggest barriers that will stop you from becoming the best you can be.

"What age would it be good to shift to one sport?"

My question in response to this question would be *"Why do you want to shift to one sport?"*

Your answer will tell you if you should, or not. If your answer is based on fear or the desire to "be the best today", it's probably not wise to shift to one sport right now.

There has not been a ton of research on the specific age that it is good to specialize. Every athlete is different, and their chronological age does not always give enough information about how your body will respond to repetitive training and the same movements over and over again.

REMEMBER THIS: you are UNIQUE! Just because something works for another athlete does NOT mean it will work for you.

I had friends who ate at McDonald's right before football games and were fine.

If I did that...

Well, let's not go there. Back to the topic:

I don't know the right age, but my best recommendation would be to wait until after you go through puberty and to make sure you are doing it for the right reasons, not because you are copying others or you are scared of falling behind. If the elite athletes we are able to look at were able to play numerous sports in high school and reach their full potential, you can too!

Elite Athletes Who Played Multiple Sports

Tom Brady: 7 Time Super Bowl Champ and 5 Time Super Bowl MVP. Tom was a baseball catcher in high school and credits his multi-sport background for developing his agility and throwing accuracy.

Kobe Bryant: 4 Time MVP and 5 Time NBA Champion. The late and great Kobe grew up playing soccer and gained footwork skills that he says contributed to his incredible agility on the court.

Serena Williams: 23 Grand Slam Women's Singles Titles. Serena and her sister Venus participated in junior tournaments for various sports to enhance their overall athleticism.

Lionel Messi: 7 Time FIFA World Soccer Player of the Year. As a young athlete, Messi played basketball in addition to soccer. This played a huge part in developing his exceptional balance and coordination on the soccer field.

LeBron James: Only Player in NBA History with 30,000 points, 10,000 rebounds, and 10,000 assists. LeBron was an exceptional football player through high school which helped him develop a multitude of skills that transferred to the court.

Jackie Joyner-Kersee: 6-Time Olympic Gold Medalist in Track and Field. In addition to her extraordinary track and field career, Jackie started four years on the UCLA women's basketball team.

Russell Wilson: Super Bowl Champion Quarterback and 9 Time Pro Bowler: Did you know that Russell was a standout baseball player growing up, drafted by the Colorado Rockies?

Michael Jordan: 6 Time NBA Champion and 6 Time Final MVP. While it did not last long, MJ's brief stint playing professional baseball revealed how valuable it is to play multiple sports.

Mia Hamm: 2 Time Olympic Gold Medalist with Team USA Women's Soccer, 2 FIFA World Cup Championships, and 4 NCAA Championships in a Row with UCLA Soccer. Mia was a multi-sport athlete playing basketball and volleyball in high school.

Wayne Gretzky: Holds the NHL Record for Goals, Assists, Points, Hat-Tricks, and Game-Winning Goals. Called the "Great One" for a reason, Wayne played lacrosse growing up which undoubtedly led to his exceptional hand-eye coordination for hockey.

Usain Bolt: Only Sprinter In Olympic History To Win 100m, 200m and 4x100m Gold Medal At 3 Consecutive Olympics. Bolt is the fastest man in the world, yet he played cricket and soccer in his early years!

Julie Ertz: Captain of the US Women's National Soccer Team and Triple Crown in the World Cup. Julie was a multi-sport athlete in high school, participating in track and field and basketball.

Javier Hernandez: Top Goal Scorer of Any Mexico National Soccer Player. Hernandez played both soccer and baseball growing up.

Michael Phelps: Most Decorated Olympian In History with 23 Gold Medals. Did you know that he played lacrosse and soccer before focusing on swimming?!?

Simone Biles: Most Decorated Gymnast in World Championship History with 30 Medals. She participated in cheerleading and enjoyed running which undoubtedly led to her impressive strength and agility.

Cristiano Ronaldo: One of the Top Soccer Players of All Time with 34 Trophies Won. Ronaldo played both soccer and basketball growing up.

Alex Honnold: The 1st Rock Climber to Free Solo a Route on El Capitan. Alex was a competitive swimmer and played soccer as a kid. While I don't encourage free solo rock climbing, I just had to include this one.

Clearly, multiple sports can lead to massive success. But what are the other benefits of playing multiple sports?

What are the negatives?

I want YOU to make this list for yourself. The implications are bigger than you may have initially thought...

PROS OF MULTIPLE SPORTS:

1.

2.

3.

4.

5.

CONS OF MULTIPLE SPORTS:

1.

2.

3.

4.

5.

2. The Link Between Mental Health Issues and Athletes Who Engage in *Excessive* Sports Training and Competition

Now that you are starting to get used to the fact that *more is not always better*, let's talk about how playing a single sport and training excessively, year round, could be what stops you in your tracks.

Sports Science Journals, Sports Psychology Literature, the National Institute of Health (NIH), numerous Sports Medicine Organizations such as the American College of Sports Medicine (ACSM), and countless books and reviews on sports psychology agree that excessive training and competition is an issue we need to discuss.

Some of the mental health issues that research shows are linked to excessive competition includes:

- Increased Stress and Anxiety
- Depression
- Burnout
- Decreased Motivation (interesting how that works)
- Sleep Disturbances
- Irritability and Mood Swings
- Decreased Self-Esteem
- Social Withdrawal

Just take a moment to assess your own mindset and emotions. Do you experience any of those?

If you do, I recommend telling your parents, coaches, and/or professionals. You don't need to struggle with those things. You can reach your full potential while remaining mentally and emotionally healthy along the way!

Nia's Story

Nia is a high level gymnast who was having feelings of depression. She was 17 years old and was just realizing that she had not come up for air in the past 13 years since stepping on the mat as a 4 year old.

Becoming all-around state champion at 6 years old was a big deal. Her parents and coaches made her feel like she was a pro athlete. This caused everyone around her to start asking the question, "How far can she go?"

She was exhausted mentally, physically, and emotionally from doing gymnastics year round and never taking time off. She was so scared of falling behind.

She finally realized that she needed to make a change. I gave her permission to, but she ultimately needed to give herself permission and believe that it was actually the best thing for her performance long term.

Nia decided to take 3 months off. After those 3 months, on her own terms, she decided to return to the sport. Only this time, she had a renewed mind, body, and passion.

During those 3 months, it's not like Nia just sat around and watched TV shows. No, she decided to work on her mindset. During those 3 months Nia and I met weekly to help her:

1. Discover the truth about who she was and why she mattered.
2. Reflect on her past and all the progress she had made as a young woman.
3. Set goals for her future- not just what she wanted to accomplish, but who she wanted to become.

4. Create a definition of winning and success for her life.
5. Learn how to understand and appreciate others for who *they* are.
6. Learn how to find the good in any situation.
7. Create a new definition of failure, one that wouldn't make it so easy for her to feel like she failed.
8. Develop a habit and attitude of gratitude- she began journaling every morning and writing down 3 things from the day before that she was thankful for

Before Nia took time off, she constantly felt stuck, like she was being *stopped* by some forces outside of her control. But once Nia realized that she was in control of some of these decisions, and she decided to prioritize her mental and physical well-being, she began to feel UNSTOPPABLE again!

Do you need to make a big decision right now so that you too can become unstoppable?

PAUSE TO REFLECT:

1. What from Nia's story stands out to me and why?
2. Out of the 8 things we worked on with Nia, which 3 would most help you become a better version of yourself?

Learn to Master Your Mindset
IN THE MOMENT

If you are going to become UNSTOPPABLE, you need to two different types of mental skills:

1. The ability to master your mindset **in the moment.**
2. The ability to master your mindset **long-term.**

In this chapter we will focus on mastering your mindset in a game-time situation.

- Imagine, you just made a costly error.

- You missed a shot you should have made, you dropped a pass you should have caught, or you overthrew your teammate.

- The game hasn't started yet, and you are feeling nervous and lacking confidence.

- You need to get locked in and focused so that you can dominate.

You need a tool to master your mindset at that exact moment. Otherwise, you are toast.

Tool #1: The Mindset Reset Tool

Every athlete needs a customized technique that is unique to them for moments where you lose focus, get frustrated, or shift into an unhelpful frame of mind.

What is the Mindset Reset Tool? A tool to reset your mindset, of course.

1. A RESET WORD.
2. A HAND SIGNAL.
3. A DEEP BREATH.

Step 1: Choose Your Word

- *Focus*
- *Unstoppable*
- *Dominate*
- *Overcome*
- *Locked-In*
- *Next Play*
- *Win*
- *Strong*
- *Courageous*
- *I've Got This*
- *Let It Go*

These are some examples of ones that other athletes have chosen. The word is less important than what the word MEANS to you. Choose one for you that has power and meaning.

Step 2: Choose a Strong Hand Signal

- *Clap once*
- *Clap twice*
- *Shake out the hands*
- *Punch your palm*
- *Slap your leg*
- *Snap your fingers*
- *Cross your fingers*
- *Wiggle your fingers*
- *Tap your head*

Again, the most important part of this is that you choose a hand signal that matches your RESET WORD. Pick a hand signal that makes you feel powerful, strong, like you can and will OVERCOME. Be unstoppable.

Step 3: Link the two together with a DEEP BREATH

Now, if you are like me, you are going to get excited about this, try it a few times, and then stop doing it.

"Successful people do repeatedly what unsuccessful people do occasionally."

Make a commitment to yourself right now that you will establish your reset tool today, and that you will use it every day.

Why? Because it works. It has worked for every single athlete that has ever done it!

To access a bonus instructional video of me teaching this, scan the QR code.

Tool #2: Advanced Visualization

You cannot be what you cannot see.

If you cannot see yourself being successful, you won't be successful.

Believing in yourself is paramount to succeeding. If you haven't believed in yourself up to this point, I want you to stop right now and remember all the times you have succeeded in the past. Write them down. If you do not take back control of your mind, it will automatically remember the times that you failed!

Before you move on, think about all the times in your past 1-2 years that you crushed it. Think about the times you were confident, the moments you succeeded, the game where you did extremely well. Go back to those times and remember them. How does it feel?

Now, we can continue.

Vision is always the front door into your best performance.

The problem is that most athletes have learned a watered down, boring version of visualization and they don't fully believe in it. Visualization that doesn't work involves one dimension- *sitting down, closing your eyes, and playing some boring movie in your mind's eye.*

That's it, and it doesn't work very well.

Advanced visualization is when you get more of your senses involved and you activate your physiology in the process!

PRE-WORK: Decide how you are going to celebrate after you are successful. See it. Feel it. Are you going to throw your arms up in a victory pose? Are you going to run to your teammate and chest bump them? Are you going to yell?

Decide on the celebration because after you visualize success, you had better celebrate it.

Step 1: Decide what you are going to visualize. Is it an offensive play? Defensive? A game winning shot? A routine at bat? The way you are going to respond to getting pulled out? The way you are going to respond to getting beat by an offensive player?

Whatever you are wanting to be more successful at is what you should visualize.

Step 2: Stand up (unless you are seated in your sport, i.e. chess player) and move like you are going somewhere. Shift your weight side to side, move your body, get in the game.

Step 3: See everything you would normally see. The fans, the stadium/atmosphere, the scoreboard, the lines painted, the basket, etc. See it all.

Step 4: Hear everything you would normally hear. The fans, coach yelling (but then, silence that). Hear your teammates cheering for you. Hear the wind blowing. Hear the bat clank against your cleats.

Step 5: Go through the event, full speed. If you are a swimmer, you better be moving those arms whether you are in the pool or not. If you are a softball player, you better be in your full blown hitting stance and execute the motion full speed.

Step 6: Celebrate.

Step 7: Do it again.

Step 8: Do it again. And again. And again! Reward what you want to repeat and repeat what you want to reward.

Visualization works.

Advanced visualization works better.

If it hasn't worked in the past, it is because you didn't work it the right way, enough times, for long enough.

Here is the other reason why Advanced Visualization is so important: *your ability to **anticipate** is your #1 competitive advantage in sports and life.*

If you can anticipate what is going to happen, such as your opponent's next move, you have the advantage every time. You will become unstoppable.

When asked what made him the best that ever played, Wayne Gretzky famously replied, *"Other players skate to where the puck is. I skate to where the puck is going."*

How do you become a better anticipator of patterns in sports?

#1: Repetition

#2: Advanced Visualization- "See where the puck is going."

#3: Repetition

Repetition leads to confidence and confidence leads to mastery.

You are one decision away from being a totally different athlete. You ARE an athlete who has the ability to anticipate. You ARE an athlete who has unbeatable grit and determination. You ARE smart, strategic, and dominant.

You've got this, I know it, and YOU know it.

Athlete, take this seriously. Decide right now to become great at anticipating!

Tool #3: In Between Points (or plays)

Before I share the "In Between The Points" mental preparation exercise, I want to make sure you are practicing like you play. Are you bringing the same level of focus and intensity to practice? If not, you need to start there. Your physical preparation matters big time. This is a big reason why many athletes are not performing as well in games as they could be.

But if you are bringing your focus and intensity to practices, then this exercise will help.

99% of your problems during games or competitions are in your head and heart rate. You are either too worked up, or too "slowed down".

You are either lacking energy, or you are *too* energized.

There was a study done on the top 100 tennis players in the world and they found that the ones who cracked the top 50 consistently did **5 things in between points** that the others did not.

1. They Walked with Purpose.

They walked fast to get pumped up and excited, and slowly if they needed to calm down and slow their heart rate.

2. They Talked With Purpose.

They knew exactly what they were going to say to themselves if they were winning, losing, in match point, etc. They had "pre-planned" self-talk.

3. They Breathed with Purpose.

Similar to the way they walked, they breathed quickly to get pumped up and excited, and slowly if they needed to calm down and slow their heart rate.

4. They Maintained Good Posture.

Ever had a coach or parent tell you to "keep your head and chest up"? Well, it works. The top 50 in the world were very serious about maintaining strong and confident posture even when things were not going well.

5. They Maintained Good Eye Contact.

In between plays or points, the best in the world always had somewhere you looked that encouraged them. Perhaps they looked at a fan in the stands, up to God, or somewhere else that was meaningful for them. But they didn't look down!

So, there you go. Three competition-tested tools to help you master your mindset in game-time, high pressure situations.

Now, let's move on and learn the 3 keys to master your mindset *long-term* so that you aren't just unstoppable in games, but so that you become unstoppable for years and years to come.

KEY #6

Think LONG-TERM

Remember, in order to become one of the rare athletes who achieves incredible success while also remaining healthy and happy along the way, you are going to need to think differently.

Unstoppable athletes think long-term. They do not play by the same rules as everyone else. Instead, they set long-term goals and have their own definition of success. They have an infinite *mindset* which keeps them from freaking out when they have one bad game, one setback, they get benched, they don't make a team, etc. They also keep a healthy perspective by reflecting on their wins and measuring their progress backwards.

I cannot change anyone except myself. And neither can you. A key to becoming unstoppable is to not let the opinions of others, nor their actions and decisions, determine *your* path.

When you decide to take back control of your mindset and decisions, you give yourself a massive boost of confidence.

Below are 3 decisions that you need to make if you are going to regain control and master your mindset:

Long-Term Decision #1: Choose Your Own Definition of Success

What does success mean to you?

Are you successful when:

- You get playing time?
- You start?
- You score a bunch of points?
- Coach gives you compliments?
- They mention you in the paper?
- You earned an all-conference award?

The problem with these things determining your success is that *they are not within your control.*

I am not saying they are bad; they aren't! They are great! But they are outcomes, not inputs.

Your mindset will be stronger immediately when you choose a definition of success that is within your control!

Here is the definition of success that a lot of the elite athletes that I coach have adopted:

Success is peace of mind which is a direct result of self-satisfaction in knowing that I did my best to become the best I was capable of becoming...

And helping as many others along the way as I possibly could.

Why does this matter?

Because if you do not choose your own definition of success and decide to stick with it NO MATTER WHAT, then your confidence is going to roller coaster up and down, up and down, every time one of those things above that are outside of your control do not happen.

Do you perform well and enjoy the game when your confidence is yo-yoing?

Of course not.

Use the space below to craft your definition:

My Definition of Success That is Within My Control Is:

Long-Term Decision #2: Choose An Infinite Mindset

There was a book written many years ago called "Finite and Infinite Games" by James Carse.

The implications of what I am about to share with you have the power to completely transform the way you think, feel, and show up in your sport. This concept has the power to free you from worry, excessive nervousness, and fear about the future.

In his book, he shares that Finite Games are games where:

1. The competitors are all known.

2. Once the game is over, it is over. There is a beginning and an end, which evokes a sense of worry and fear that the game will come to an end, and you might not win.
3. There is a winner and a loser. In the finite game mindset, there is no benefit to losing. Only regret and disappointment.

These descriptions beg the question, if you have been spending your entire career viewing your sport as a *finite* game, could that be why you've experienced so much anxiety, fear, and worry? Could this finite mindset be responsible for you playing tense and performing with a mental limp?

Infinite games, on the other hand, are games where:

1. The point is to keep the game going. You do so by improving things, finding the good in the challenges, enjoying the people you are playing with, and doing your part in creating team unity.
2. There is no real "end" to it. Sure, each chapter, such as high school or college sports, will come to an end. But that isn't the point. The point is that you love playing the game and want to continue.
3. Temporary setbacks or defeats are not a big deal because the game never ends. You are not *racing against an arbitrary clock*, but rather you are learning and growing every day.

So, have you been viewing your sport as a finite or infinite game? Why do you think you've viewed your sport this way?

What if you decided today to shift your mindset and start viewing sports as the Infinite Games that they truly are?

I know what will happen. You will stop sweating the small stuff. You will be more relaxed. You will be more calm, cool, and collected. And you will perform better in the short-term.

When you think *long-term*, you play better *short-term*. It's a beautiful thing!

Long-Term Decision #3: Stop Beating Yourself Up For Not Being Further Along, and Start Building Your Confidence By Measuring Your Progress Backwards

In my book, ATHLETE! 7 Mindset Hacks to Dominate in Sports and Life, I shared the concept about progress and motivation.

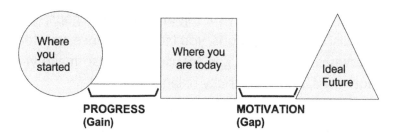

Do you constantly obsess over your future dreams (college sports, getting a scholarship, getting noticed, going pro)?

Do you spend way more time focusing on how far you fall short than on how far you have come?

Do not beat yourself up. You should feel encouraged knowing that there is a better way…

Oftentimes, parents and coaches unintentionally cause you to focus more on your mistakes than you do on your successes. They are constantly pointing out how to be better, how to stop making mistakes, and how to get to the next level.

This is not bad, but it cannot be your main focus if you are going to master a positive, healthy, high-performing mindset.

When you focus on where you've grown, your "gains", you feel amazing, confident, accomplished, happy, and successful. These are all the emotions you need in order to succeed in reaching your ideal future!

However, when you focus too much on how far you currently fall short of your big dreams, your "gaps," you feel discouraged, anxious, you lack confidence, you feel overwhelmed. Being "gap focused" can also make you motivated, but it is a tricky balance.

Before we move on, take a moment to reflect on what you have accomplished. Use the space below or in your workbook to answer the following questions.

Write down 3-5 things you have made progress on in the last year. What have you accomplished? How have you grown as a player? As a person?

To help you get started, here's an example:

Example:

1. *I am a better shooter now.*
2. *I took more shots this year instead of playing passive.*
3. *I got quicker.*
4. *I proved to myself that I can finish a game.*
5. *I developed the habit of asking coach for help.*

Now, it is your turn. Go ahead and list your improvements in the space below:

1.

2.

3.

4.

5.

How do you feel after doing that exercise?

When I meet with athletes, they usually say things like:

"I feel more confident, like I actually CAN achieve the bigger and better future I am hoping for."

"I feel proud and accomplished."

"Better. I feel better."

It is not rocket science, it is a habit. And if you've been practicing the wrong habit (gap thinking) for years, it is going to take some effort to break that habit.

Progress and Motivation

You can begin practicing the habit of being satisfied with progress *and* motivated to work towards your big goals today. The next few exercises are designed to help you imagine the possibilities and cultivate a new mindset. But nothing will happen unless you roll up your sleeves and make the choice to change.

Your Accomplishments Exercise

List out the 5 things you have accomplished up to this point in your life that you are most proud of:

1.

2.

3.

4.

5.

What does your bigger and better exciting future look like? Draw a picture or write about that in the space below.

Be sure to include your big goals, where you see yourself in the next 5-10 years, and who you want to become as a person along the way. For example, do you see yourself as a motivating leader, a stronger and more resilient person, a more resourceful person?

The Habits

Building new habits is possible, but they take time and a voracious focus. There are varying opinions about how long it takes to create a new habit. Some say it takes 21 days, while others say it takes 90 days. Whatever length of time it takes you, let me encourage you to be intentional and do what is needed to create new habits that will help you take back control and become the best you.

Track and field Olympian Jim Ryun once said, "Motivation is what gets you started. Habit is what keeps you going."

With that truth in mind, let's walk through some exercises you can do to create new habits while feeling proud, positive, and accomplished after every season, at the end of each week, and at the end of each day.

Hint: The things you write out do not have to be HUGE things in order for you to achieve a positive mindset.

Write down the 3-5 things you made progress during your last sports season.

From last week: write down 3-5 things you did well, that you made progress on, that you accomplished, etc.

From yesterday: write down 3-5 things that went well, that you did well, that you made progress on, that you accomplished, etc.

Do not skip this exercise. It's a key piece to taking back control, restoring your passion, and to feeling proud of yourself again.

Now you know the 3 keys to mastering your mindset and you are ready to implement these into your everyday habits. Go back and read this chapter again if you need to. This one is paramount to your long-term success.

But speaking of habits, let's talk about one of the most important habits of all: *Sharpening Your Ax*.

Watch My Free Keynote Presentation of the 3 Keys to Mastering Your Mindset

Sharpen Your Ax,
Get 1% Better Everyday

If you are going to reach the top of your game, you must develop the habit of sharpening your ax. Unstoppable athletes did not become unstoppable overnight. They developed the habit of getting 1% better every day, which doesn't always look flashy or make SportsCenter Top 10!

Let's be honest. The crowd is not going to cheer for you for taking time to sharpen your ax. That is because sharpening your ax is what happens *before* you step into the spotlight and have consistent, all-star performances.

The Story

There was a tree-cutting competition in Cotoberry, Michigan. Josh Devoir was the clear favorite to win.

For months, he had been beating the rest of the competition by a landslide. It seemed that Josh was the *ultimate definition of success.*

The day came for the competition and a new challenger, Terry Sharper, made his way onto the scene. The difference with this particular event was that the trees were about 60% bigger than they were in normal competitions.

As Josh typically did, he peered over at the new guy and with a look of pity and said, "You can just go home now, Terry. Don't waste your time."

The competition began and Josh, with lightning speed and tenacity, began taking huge hacks at the tree with his ax.

Crack! Crack! Crack! Josh was so powerful and skilled it was like watching perfection.

5 minutes and 30 seconds into the competition, Terry was gone.

"Rookie!" Josh said to himself.

3 minutes later, Terry was back on the scene smacking away at the tree.

The only problem was that Josh was halfway done and Terry was only at 30% completion.

5 minutes and 30 seconds after returning, Terry vanished again.

"Ohhhh this is like taking candy from a baby. Some people just aren't built for this!" Josh smiled as he exclaimed.

At that moment, someone in the crowd nudged a fellow spectator and said, "Does Josh look a little fatigued to you?"

3 minutes later, Terry was back. He looked better than when he started, His posture was strong, his swings were perfect, and he was even smiling and connected with the fans as he was chopping away.

Josh was at 79% completion, Terry 71%. It was getting close. But how could that be?

Josh had taken twice as many swings and had been working for ~50% longer than Terry had been!

Terry looked at Josh and gave him a nod as he smiled. Josh's swing frequency was down significantly. His power was clearly diminishing. Terry set his ax down gently and walked away one final time.

3 minutes later he returned, picked up his ax, and took 10 final, powerful hacks at the tree. The crowd watched in awe as the last 3 hacks toppled the tree over.

"8...9....10...timber!!!!!!"

The crowd went wild.

Josh fell to his knees. He was exhausted. He was defeated. He had placed all his eggs in this basket. He had trained 7 days a week, 30 days a month, 365 days a year for this. How could he have lost!?!

It was impossible to even imagine that Terry had trained as long and hard as he had!

And then, Josh noticed something.

Terry's ax looked wildly different from his...

It was still sharp.

"What were you doing every time you left the scene?" Josh asked Terry.

"Sharpening my ax of course," Terry said in an obvious tone.

How To Sharpen Your Ax:

Sharpening your ax is taking time off of playing your sport in order to focus on **recovery, habits to renew your passion, strength and speed training, skill development, strategy and watching film, etc.**

Just as your muscles grow *in between workouts*, your abilities as an athlete grow *in between* performances. But only if you do the right things, frequently enough, for long enough, to sharpen your ax.

Two words come to mind when I think about the way an elite athlete sharpens his or her ax:

Consistency + Intensity = UNSTOPPABLE

The two reasons most athletes never become unstoppable and reach their full potential is a result of either a lack of *consistency* or a lack of *intensity*.

Consistency is how frequently we do something over time. Intensity represents *how* we do something. Consistent intensity is how frequently we do something with peak focus and effort.

Your speed, strength, power, and conditioning training comes to mind.

Consistency:

Have you ever gotten really motivated after going to watch a college game?

Or maybe you get really motivated after a big showcase where college coaches are coming to watch.

You decided *that day*, "I'm going to be consistent!"

But then, your motivation ran dry.

You must decide every single day that no matter how "motivated" you feel or don't feel, you will remain consistent.

Consistent stretching. Consistent with your water intake. Consistent with putting your phone down 1 hour before bed and getting a good night sleep. Consistent in all the areas that matter most to you.

Motivation gets you going, habits keep you growing. You must decide that you will stay committed and consistent long after the *feeling* you had when you initially became motivated, has left you. This is key to becoming the best you can be.

- If you stick to quality strength training for one year two-three times per week, you will put yourself into an elite class of athletes.
- If your sport requires amazing endurance and you follow a consistent plan to get a little better

and a little faster every day, every week, you will become unbeatable.

- If you can commit to studying for your tests and doing tutoring for one full semester consistently, you'll blow your parents away with your grades.

Ask yourself today, "How committed and consistent have I been over the last year? Not just the last 3 weeks, but the last year?"

Consistency will get you far, but what exactly are you being consistent with? Do you need to upgrade *how* you are doing what you're doing?

Intensity:

When I went to college my freshman year to play basketball, I thought I was in great shape. After all, I had worked out and played basketball five or six days a week for the entire summer, and for a long time leading up to that summer.

I was very *consistent*.

When I got there, I noticed something about the *way* the upperclassmen were training, conditioning, recovering, and doing their skill development. Their *intensity* was way different.

How do you *hone your how?*

These guys were doing drills in a way that I had never seen, at an intensity I did not know existed. In addition, they had their teammates filming them during their drills. I thought this was a little crazy and over the top.

That is what people say who really don't want to change, put in more work, or do what is needed to become UN-STOPPABLE. They say things like, "That's over the top."

If you want to become a world-class swimmer, avoid plateaus, experience *continual improvement*, and continually level up your results, it will take *far more* than swimming five days a week for two hours a day, year after year.

In fact, you will probably want to do less, better, over a long period of time.

PAUSE TO REFLECT:

1. What would it look like for me to raise my intensity, lower my duration, and stay more consistent over long periods of time?
2. What do I struggle more with, consistency or intensity?
3. Do I take intentional time to sharpen my ax? That is, do I consistently prioritize rest and recovery? Do I renew my passion and energy by taking time off? Do I invest time and energy to repair and rebuild my body after tough seasons/games/etc.?
4. If yes, what do I do that would be considered "sharpening my ax"? How do I approach getting 1% better every day?

5. What changes do I need to make to be "sharper" so that I can remain healthy and become UN-STOPPABLE?

KEY #8

Balance Patience and Persistence

Have you ever heard the concept of working smart *and* working hard?

That is what balancing patience and persistence is all about. It is about becoming an athlete who is patient with your own progress and development. It is about recognizing that we get better *daily*, not in a day.

But it is also important to have persistence when we feel the resistance.

Consider lifting weights:

When you are lifting weights, the only way to get stronger is if you push yourself past the resistance of those last couple of reps. The majority of the strength you gain happens during those last few reps!

This is *persistence.*

But do your muscles grow when you are lifting weights? No.

They grow when you are resting.

This is *patience.* This is *working smart.*

Persistence continues to help you reach your full potential as you engage in this habit week after week, month after month, and year after year.

Taking Time Off + Intentionally Sharpening Your Ax = Growth.

You do this by 1 day off every week, 1 week off every season, and 1 season off every year.

Balancing patience and persistence is the most important step to becoming an unstoppable athlete. You need time and space to rest, rebuild, and repair your *physical body.*

Taking this time off gives you time to level up your physical strength, speed, and explosiveness by doing *dedicated* strength training.

"I thought I was supposed to strength train in season?"

Yes, the benefits of training in season far outweigh the benefits of *not* strength training in season.

But don't fool yourself- where attention goes, energy flows. When you have the self-discipline to push *pause* on playing in practices, games, and tournaments for a period of time, you will see a greater increase in your explosiveness, strength, speed, and agility. We have seen this work for literally thousands of athletes who train with us.

If you decide to try to "do it all" and you exhaust yourself with practice, games, and cardio while simultaneously trying to build muscle and power, you will hit a plateau.

And remember, taking time off from high-pressure and high-intensity competition also gives you dedicated time to invest in hobbies, relationships, and other things that are most important to you.

Lastly, having a consistent rhythm of time off gives you the capacity to restore something that most of us in the sports community do not really talk about because it is so hard to quantify...

Your passion.

PAUSE TO REFLECT:

1. Would you describe yourself as more patient, or more persistent with your own progress?
2. At this stage in your career as an athlete, which do you need more of? Persistence, patience, or both? Why?

KEY #9

Ignite Your Passion

Rebecca hobbled into her Mindset Session on crutches.

"Rebecca! What happened!?" I *tried* to calmly ask her.

"I tore my right ACL, coach. This is the worst thing that could have happened to me. I am a junior and this is the big season for me. It's over."

Rebecca was a stud soccer player who 3 years prior had torn her left ACL. She had been specializing in only soccer since she was in 7th grade.

Rebecca and I met every other week for Mindset Training to help her get through this with a positive attitude and to help her stay laser focused on finding the silver lining. Unfortunately, it looked bleak as the months rolled by.

About 9 months later she was beginning to return to non-contact play. She was ahead of schedule.

One day after school, Rebecca walked into the gym and smiled. She said, "I found it. I found the silver lining!"

"What is it?" I asked.

"My passion. To be honest, I haven't been excited or passionate about playing in the last three years. I had no clue how much I was missing that. I am doing things with the ball that I haven't done in years, and I am only 9 months post-op. I needed to lose soccer again to miss it. It feels good to want to practice instead of feeling like I *have to*."

I was happy for her but also troubled as I asked myself, *"Isn't there a better way to keep your passion high?"*

Avoid the 5 Passion Killers

"Passion is a huge prerequisite to winning. It makes you willing to jump through hoops, go through all the ups and downs and everything in between to reach your goal."

— Kerri Walsh Jennings

Why are some elite, professional, and Olympic level athletes able to get to the top of their game and stay there for longer than others?

Does the money keep them passionate?

Probably not. Money cannot make you a mentally tough, healthy, happy, and high-performing athlete.

How to Keep Your Passion High

1. Don't lose it to begin with.

We know how burnout and loss of passion occurs. *One practice, one game, one day, one week, one month, one season, one year at a time.*

The 5 Passion Killers:

- Having no **balance,** no hobbies, and no life outside of sport
- Not being able to use your **strengths** and **gifts** in your sport

- Not receiving enough **positive praise** or **recognition**
- Not having **connection** with our teammates
- Not having **goals** or a **compelling vision** for the future

Difficult circumstances do not in and of themselves lead to burnout or loss of passion. It's a combination of those five things above, which are all within our control.

Remember, there is no greater detriment to your passion, your energy, and your JOY than saying *yes* to every opportunity that comes your way.

PAUSE TO REFLECT:

1. Which of the 5 killers are currently sucking your passion dry?
    a. Having no **balance,** no hobbies, and no life outside of sport
    b. Not being able to use your **strengths** and **gifts** in your sport
    c. Not receiving enough **positive praise** or **recognition**
    d. Not having **connection** with our teammates
    e. Not having **goals** or a **compelling vision** for the future
2. Think about what you need to stop, start, or continue doing to keep passion high and write about that in the space below.

Stay Fresh By Maximizing Ultradian Rhythms

Earlier in the book I talked about ultradian rhythms. What are they and why do they matter?

Picture this: your body has this cool built-in rhythm, like a secret code, running in cycles of about 90 to 120 minutes.

It's like a playlist, but for your energy levels. If the first 10 chapters of this book did not convince you to take a good, hard look at your current schedule and make changes to optimize your health and performance, then this will.

Imagine these ultradian cycles as your body's way of telling you, "Hey, it's go-time!"

During the high-energy phase, you're like a superhero—fast reflexes, sharp thinking, in the zone, and absolutely locked-in.

But, just like superheroes need their downtime, there's a cool-down phase too. That's when your body says, "Alright, time for a breather."

FIGURE 2
THE ULTRADIAN PERFORMANCE RHYTHM

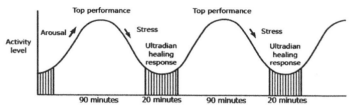

Adapted from: Rossi, EL: *The 20 Minute Break*. Tarcher Putnam, New York, 1991 p. 12

Getting Practical

Ultradian rhythms can differ from person to person, but 90 minutes seems to be the absolute maximum amount of time that a person can truly sustain peak performance. And even that long is questionable.

Example: If your practices last 90+ minutes, you would actually get more accomplished *and* feel more energized afterwards if you took a 15-20 minute break somewhere in the middle. I will tell your coaches this in the Coach and Parent Edition of this book.

Does this concept apply to my personal workouts? What about my studying?

The concept of ultradian rhythms can be applied to any area of your life. Remember, you were created to sprint and then rest, sprint and then rest!

Study for 60 minutes and then take a 20 minute walk.

Workout for 60 minutes and then take a 20 minute break before you do conditioning. The key here is to resist the temptation to "power through" when your mind and body really need to break!

You are not weak for doing this. You are wise!

Maximizing Your Weekly Routine

If you are going to be an athlete who thrives in sports and life, you need a day of rest.

A day where you literally do not pick up a ball, study film, or do anything that would be considered "trying to get better." The point of the rest day is to *get better by doing less.*

Remember in chapter 7 when we concluded that your muscles get bigger *not* when you are training and playing, but rather when you are resting?

A day of rest will do more for your performance than an extra day of hustling and grinding. It will be just enough time off to make you excited to go out the next day and practice.

When was the last time you were genuinely excited to practice? If you want to get a little bit of that excitement back, try intentionally depriving yourself, just for a day, from your sport.

You can either choose to do this, or like Rebecca and her ACL tear, you can be forced to take time off. Choose wisely!

Sit with this concept for a little while. Reflect on it. How much performance, passion, joy, and success are you leaving on the table by *not* taking one true day off of sports?

Take Action and Forge Your Path to Sustained Greatness

Athlete, my final question for you is, *what are you going to do?* Information + Application = Transformation.

Becoming unstoppable is going to require massive, consistent action! This includes owning your schedule and prioritizing what matters most, ignoring the lies and running your own race, building habits of mental toughness and high performance, building different skills through multiple sports, mastering your short and long-term mindset, balancing patience and persistence, sharpening your ax every day, igniting and keeping your passion high, and maximizing your circadian rhythms.

It sounds like a lot. But you don't need to do it all in a day. Athletes who have become UNSTOPPABLE didn't just one day wake up that way. They became that way one habit, day, week, month, season, and year at a time.

ACTION TIME: This is why I want you to download the Free Unstoppable Athlete ACTION Guide and do it with your team. Download the link below and then send your coach or teammate the other link below so that they can grab their copies.

Yesterday is history. Tomorrow is a mystery. All you can do is the best that you can do *today*.

The path to reaching your full potential is within your reach. Download the Action Guide, gather your teammates, and start becoming unstoppable TODAY!

You do not have to be perfect. You just need to be bold and take action. You've got this, and I am here for you and rooting for you every step of the way.

Your friend and coach,

Coach Andrew J Simpson

<u>Your Review Could Help ONE MORE Athlete Go From No Belief, to Fully Confident.</u>

If you enjoyed the book, would you leave a review?

Next Step: DOWNLOAD YOUR
UNSTOPPABLE ATHLETE ACTION GUIDE!

Acknowledgements

The Lord for giving me experiences, ideas, and creative solutions to help young men and women become the leaders they were created to be.

Shaun Smithson, for always inspiring and challenging me to grow and become a better leader. Thank you for your commitment to excellence, for the way you serve student-athletes and their families, and for your early and impactful feedback on this book.

A special shoutout to the entire PFP team of DOFI's, coaches, and leaders who serve, love, and inspire our student-athletes every single day. You are life-changers and I am blessed to have the opportunity to call you teammates.

Made in the USA
Las Vegas, NV
16 December 2024